Teach Yourself Stitch Craft and Dressmaking

Pattern Making and Drafting Layout: Volume III

Making Your Own Patterns for Dress Designing

I0435475

Dueep Jyot Singh

Learning Series

Mendon Cottage Books

JD-Biz Publishing

Our books are available at

1. Amazon.com
2. Barnes and Noble
3. Itunes
4. Kobo
5. Smashwords
6. Google Play Books

Download Free Books!

http://MendonCottageBooks.com

Table of Contents

Introduction

The first two books in our series have given you information about the basics of stitch craft, and how you are going to measure the figure properly so that you can start setting out your drafting pattern.

Drafting is the method with which you are going to draw the pattern of a garment, a given measurement on a piece of paper. Proper drafting is a systematic method which involves a number of steps. Some of the measurements are going to be lengthwise and some of them are going to be widthwise.

Proper drafting is going to depend on three important factors. The first is of course the proper layout, proper pattern making and after that, the cutting of the cloth properly.

So if you do not know the basics of proper drafting, and the layout of the design, you are going to have great trouble making up the pattern with just haphazard and topsy-turvy knowledge. When I was a child, I used to see plenty of experienced tailors who just took a couple of measurements, with their inch tape and with their eyes. After that they did some mathematical calculations in the air with their fingers, and noted down some numbers on a piece of paper. After that, it was fascinating the way they just picked up a pair of heavy shears, folded the cloth so that the lower part was facing towards them.

And then they picked up a piece of tailor's chalk, held down the cloth with something heavy so that it did not wrinkle up, took their tape measurements, and measured out the cloth properly. After that they did the cutting and then they gave the stitching work to their underlings.

Hopefully, after we read this book, I and you are going to be so proficient in the basics of grafting, that we are going to understand each and every line on a drafting pattern and exactly what it means.

For this, of course, we will need to know all about proper drafting, the proper layout of the cloth, and making patterns.

So let us start with drafting.

What is the difference between drafting and laying out the pattern? Drafting is the drawing out of the pattern on a piece of paper. Laying out the pattern is cutting out the pieces of paper, according to the drafted design and then laying out the different pieces of paper properly on the cloth. After that we are going to cut the cloth, according to the pattern.

Drafting

The ability to design a dress with the help of lines and understanding the process is known as drafting. Every garment out there is going to have a different drafting design. You cannot make a pair of trousers, with a bodice design nor can a pinafore design be used to design a blouse.

However, there are some basic designs which can be adapted and once you know all about them, you can do the designs of other clothes of that same type, by just a little bit of adding, subtracting, multiplying, and dividing.

Drafting is made up of straight lines. It is also made up of circular lines for which we normally use French curves and other drafting implements and tools.

There are some lines which are going to be used in your draft, as basic lines, which are common with every single design.

However, these designs are going to be modified by adding or removing some extra lines around these basics, depending on the fashion and the garment which has to be made.

For example, if your drafting is of a bodice, the neck, shoulder, and chest measurement is going to be in the basic design. However, you can modify the shape of the neck into a circle, deep cut, square, or any other design depending on the requirements of the wearer. In the same manner, I can cut a pair of trousers when I know the basic measurements and according to the dictates of fashion, I am going to put a pocket either on the belt line, or on the pleats, or even on the knees. If I wish, I can pepper the trousers with lots of pockets and make them bellbottoms, flared, narrow, leggings, stovepipe trousers, and whatever else I wish by either adding some fabric or removing it in the design.

So once you know all about the basic math with which to calculate the basic measurements, you are going to begin drafting in a systematic and methodical manner. Once that has been done to your satisfaction, you can cut the garments to your own requirements and stitch them.

Tips While Drafting

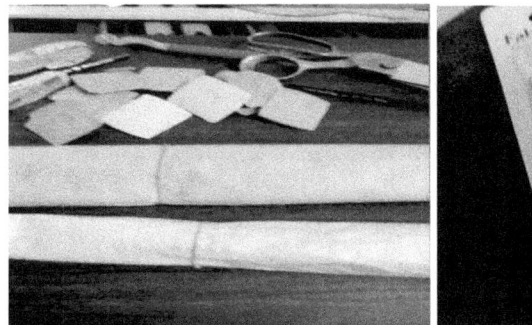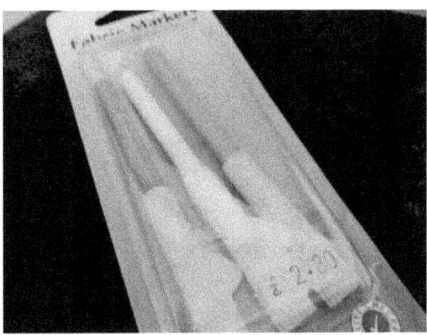

Some basic tools including an inch tape, an eraser, 2 pencils, one tracing wheel, a good pair of scissors, brown paper, tracing paper, and Tailor's chalks in different colors.

Make sure that the basic drafting is done with full measurements on a long and wide enough piece of paper. For drafting, you are going to need a sharp and dark pencil, a good eraser, some French curves for the armholes and necklines, measuring tape, and of course paper sheets. After that, you are going to need a good pair of shears in order to cut the patterns out properly after you have marked them out.

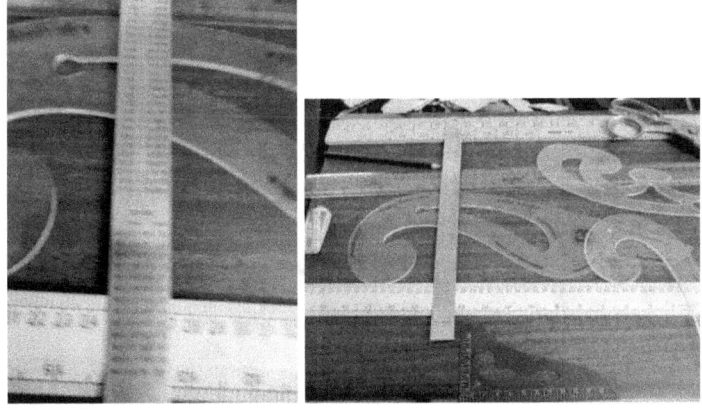

French curves and rulers, including an L-shaped wooden ruler.

You may want to do some practice cutting on a flat surface, either on your dining room table, or on the ground like I do. The dimensions of the tabletop should be around 48" x 30", which means that you have plenty of space to move around, when you are drafting the design.

A tailor's square is a wooden square with one arm of 12 inches and the other arm 24 inches or 21 inches long, depending on your requirements.

A good measuring tape is used for taking measurements as well as for drafting the diagrams so that you do not make any mistakes. It is basically going to be 60 inches long and half an inch wide with a metal strip of 3 inches on one side. Your tape is going to be marked in centimeters and inches together so that it can facilitate a measurement conversion from one system to another with just one glance.

Tailors chalks come in different colors, so make sure that the contrast but light colored chalk is used, which does not leave diagram marks on your cloth. Also have a light brush in order to brush off the marks after the cutting has been done.

The marking is always going to be done on the wrong side of the fabric. You would not want all that beautiful, luxurious black velvet fabric marked with pink or white or blue tailors chalk would you?

So the first thing you are going to is try out some practice sessions. If you can draw a straight line, you are on your way to drafting your own patterns.

At tailoring schools, you are going to use a cloth with a little bit of nap on it for practicing. This is known as Melton cloth, but as I do not have that cloth I will be using just ordinary paper.

Remember to recognize the proper lines which are necessary for your design before you start practicing on a piece of paper or drawing paper. You can start the initial drawings on a smaller scale, especially if you are just using a newspaper. Try a half scale in the initial stages.

The basic designs are for normal figures. As you gain experience, you are going to look at designs for abnormal figures. The final pattern is going to be made with full measurements on a large brown sheet of paper. This is either made on a scale measurement/full measurement.

Scale measurement actually is the measurement taken after some mathematical calculations based on a formula. It was explained in volume II, where you are going to calculate the depth of scye and body wise measurements.

Incidentally, I use a triangular set square instead of an inch tape, when I am making my final design on the brown paper. Not only is it easily movable, but it is sturdier and I can mark the points off the width and the breadth, as and when necessary.

You can also use a geometry divider with a pencil attached in order to make the circular designs of the French curve.

Remember that the perfect fitting of a garment is going to depend upon the drafting and the pattern. That is why it is very necessary that apart from drafting you know a bit about the right needles for your sewing machine, – I use a 14 – but it is going to depend on the cloth, and also the basic finishing stitches like hemming and so forth.

Also, after you have made the basic draft lines, any other lines can be made either in dashes or in dots. These are going to include dart lines, stitch lines, fold lines, and other important lines which you are normally going to see in a pattern that you have bought.

These are known as pattern markings.

Pattern Markings

Grainline – the line with arrows is going to indicate the straight grain of the fabric. You are going to put the line on an even distance from the finished edge – selvage.

Place on fold. Here you are going to place this line on the fold of the fabric.

Cutting line – for cutting.

Seam line – for sewing.

Seam allowance – the distance between cutting and the seam line is usually 1.5 cm.

Notches are used for matching the pattern pieces properly.

Cut 1 or **Cut 2** tells you how many times each piece has to be cut.

To be faced/to be interfaced means that there is no separate pattern piece included in the pattern design envelope for facing and interfacing.

You can use the same piece for cutting the garment section, the facing and interfacing.

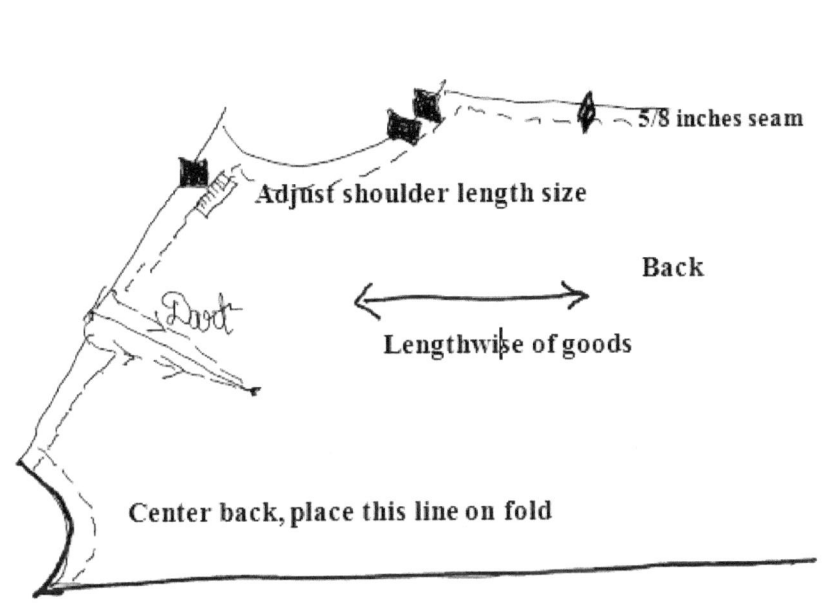

5/8 inches seam

Adjust shoulder length size

Back

Lengthwise of goods

Center back, place this line on fold

Knowing More about Scale Measurements

I touched a bit upon this topic in volume II, but here is more extended information on scale measurement. This is a scientific way in which you can reduce or extend the largest or the smallest pattern.

As tailoring is an industry in which one pattern is modified into either a larger size or a smaller size, according to the requirement of the consumers, drafting is done extensively with a little bit of calculation. For example, if we are using ½ scale, that means all the measurements in the draft is going to be half of the original measures. In the same manner, you can use 1/3, 1/4 and 1/6 scale measurements for practice before you start drafting out your final pattern.

Here is a table for reference, with which you can take the information about different scale measurements at a glance. You may want to mark out some important measurement in bold, and put it in your drafting diary.

Table for Different Scale Measurements

Chest measurement	Scale parts				
In inches	½	1/3	¼	1/6	1/12
20	10	6 5/8	5	3 3/8	1 5/8
21	10 ½	7	5 ¼	3 ½	1 ¾
22	11	7 3/8	5 ½	3 5/8	1 7/8
23	11 ½	7 7/8	5 ¾	3 7/8	1 7/8

24	12	8	6	4	2
25	12 ½	8 3/8	6 ¼	4 ¼	2 1/8
26	13	8 5/8	6 ½	4 3/8	2 ¼
27	13 ½	9	6 ¾	4 ½	2 ¼
28	14	9 3/8	7	4 ¾	2 3/8
29	14 ½	9 3/4	7 1/4	4 7/8	2 ½
30	15	10	7 ½	5	2 ½
31	15 ½	10 3/8	7 ¾	5 3/8	2 ½
32	16	10 5/8	8	5 3/8	2 5/8
33	16 ½	11	8 ¼	5 ½	2 ¾
34	17	11 3/8	8 ½	5 ¾	2 7/8
35	17 ½	11 ¾	8 ¾	5 7/8	3
36	18	12	9	6	3
37	18 ½	12 3/8	9 ¼	6 ¼	3 1/8
38	19	12 5/8	9 ½	6 3/8	3 ¼
39	19 ½	13	9 ¾	6 ½	3 ¼
40	20	13 1/3	10	6 ¾	3 3/8

41	20 ½	13 ¾	10 ¼	6 7/8	3 ½
42	21	14	10 ½	7	3 ½
43	21 ½	14 3/8	10 ¾	7 1/4	3 5/8

Method of Scale Calculation

Once you have the different chest measurements, a little bit of applied math is going to help you get the measurement of any portion of the body, in a normal figure, and this is used globally.

18 – 28 inches

1. If you are scaling 18 inches – 28 inches chest measurements, 1/3 of the chest or the seat measurements + 5 inches or 1/3 + 12 .5 cm is used as a basic scale. The final number is called the scale.

2. The moment you get this scale, you are going to get the shoulder and body rise measurements by halving this number.

Let us do a practice session. The chest measurement is 28 inches. One third of 28 is 28 divided by 3 which according to our table is 9 3/8 inches. This is our scale. Half of this number is going to be the body rise measurement and the shoulder measurement.

25 – 28 inches

When you come to the last 3 inches, 25 – 28 inches, you can half the chest and add 2 inches more. [1/2 +5 . 0 cm]. The scale which we are going to get with this measurement is going to be halved [divided by 2] to get the body rise measurement and the shoulder measurement.

29 inches – 36 inches

When the chest measurement comes within this range, you are going to take the scale by dividing the chest measurement by 1/3 and then add 6 inches

[15 cm] to the number. This is going to give you a final scale. For example, 36 inches divided by 3 = 12 +6= 18 inches.

The shoulder and the body rise measurements should be 18 divided by 2= 9 inches.

More Than 36 Inches Chest Measurement

These are for bodybuilders and Hollywood starlets. You are going to divide the chest measurement by 1/3 and add 6 inches [15 cm] and by dividing the end result scale by 2, you are going to get the shoulder measurements, which should be reasonable in an normally proportioned body.

Special Tips

Just imagine somebody with an overinflated chest with measurements more than 45 inches. Under such circumstances, the shoulder measurement should never exceed 20 inches.

I spoke about the importance of scales in measuring in the second volume. We are touching on other standard measurement points which are going to come into use.

Naturally, every measurement is going to differ according to the physical structure of the person being measured. That is why standard measurements include the **height, shoulders, cervical height**, which is from the nape of the neck to the ground –**cervical to knee**, which is from the nape of the neck to the back of the knee. After that, you are going to measure the vertical trunk which starts from the right shoulder's middle across the crotch and then crossing the stomach and the chest to the right shoulder. This is a circular measurement. The **vertical back measurement** is going to start from the middle of the shoulder and the arm. It to the middle of the other shoulder and armpit – this is also called the **across back.**

Then comes the chest measurement, neck to waist, which starts from the nape of the neck to the back of your waist. The waist is the area between the chest and the hip. This is measured in a circular measurement. If there is no clearly demarcated waist line because of a stout and thick figure, just stand naturally and allow your arms to fall in their natural positions.

The portion where your elbows touch the torso is where you are going to measure the waist.

The hip measurement is taken from the upper portion of the hip about 5 – 7 inches below the waist.

The **thigh girth** is taken on the most developed portion of the thigh in a circular measurement.

The shoulder and the arm measurements are taken together from the neck base to the shoulder and then from the end of the shoulder to the end of the arm, beginning of wrist depending on how long you want the sleeve.

Also make sure that all the main lines in a pattern are drawn boldly and clearly. The extra lines are drawn with a lighter touch. However, all of them should be clearly legible.

Like I said before, the drafting is going to be done on the wrong side of the cloth. In the first volume, I talked about the proper way in which you could fold the cloth, depending on the design.

The fold line, in a pattern should always be along the grain lengthwise. Crosswise folding is only done when there is no nap in the material or if the design demands it.

Remember that when you are cutting out the shoulder, the cloth is going to be folded lengthwise and then widthwise. That is because you will have to cut the shoulders of the shirt in such a manner that both the layers are cut properly otherwise, if the folding is wrong, the shoulder curve is not going to match at the back.

Common Terms Used In Drafting

Here are some common terms, which you are going to find in your drafting patterns, and they are global.

Terms with meaning	Abbreviations/symbols
Chest for children and men	CH
Bust for women	B
Waist for men and women	W
Hip region for women and children	H
Seat/hip region for men	S
Yoke or across back	Y/AB
Neck	N
Across chest	A.CH
The space from DART to DART	D to D
Shoulder to the dart, or from shoulder to the nipple.	S to D

Natural waist – from the shoulder to the waist.	N W
Length of sleeve – from shoulder to the required length	S. Lt.
The bottom of the sleeve	S. B.
The knee	Knee
The bottom of trousers	B. [hey, you are going to say this has the same abbreviation as the bust. But then when you are cutting out trousers, use some logic. You are not going to be measuring the bust anywhere around the ankles!]
Leg length – measurements from the inner portion of the leg, from the crotch/fork to the end of the leg.	L. Lt.
Round	R
Full-length	F.Lt.
Centerpoint – this is normally placed either on the neck or on the shoulder.	C. P.
Weft – the weave of the cloth, widthwise.	Weft
Warp- the weave of the cloth lengthwise.	Warp.

Drafting of Upper Body Garments

We are now going to start step-by-step drafting of the garments, so all the diagrams I am going to show here are how we do the systematic drafting on either ordinary paper or brown paper, depending on what you have on hand.

I did my drafting practice on newspapers with a really dark sketch pen , so I did not have to worry much when I made mistakes, drafted out wrong measurements and had to repeat the lines again and again, because I had not drawn them systematically.

1. This block pattern is used to draft shirts, bush shirts, frocks, blouses, and all the garments you wear on your upper torso.

Step 1
Measure 5 cm away from the edge of the paper and draw a full-length straight line

AB/2

1

B   Step 2 make the bust/ chest line

N. W/W
                     Step 3   make the natural waist/waistline.

H
                     Step 4 - make the hip line

F.Lt   /bottom line   Step 5- full length or bottom line

Now we come to the next part, shaping of the armhole line. The armhole line is going to be extended from 1 in the same direction as you extended the bust, hip, waist, and bottom line. After that, draw a line downwards to meet the bust line. And then draw another line downwards attaching the bust, natural waist, hip and bottom line.

So now we have the basic 5 lines which are going to make up every block pattern. The most important one, of course is the second one - the chest/bust measurement. The armhole line is the calculated measurement +1/4 inches.

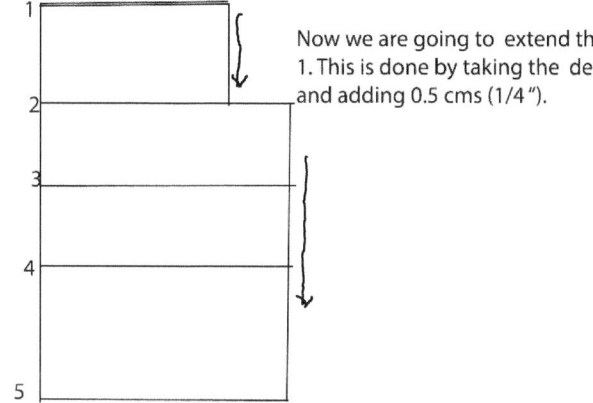

Now we are going to extend the armscye measurement from 1. This is done by taking the depth of arm scye measurement and adding 0.5 cms (1/4 ").

Drafting for Lower Body Garments

The draft given below is just a basic draft with just some labels so that you can see how trousers are drafted. This is not a final draft. We are going to learn about it as we get more experienced and start making block drafts.

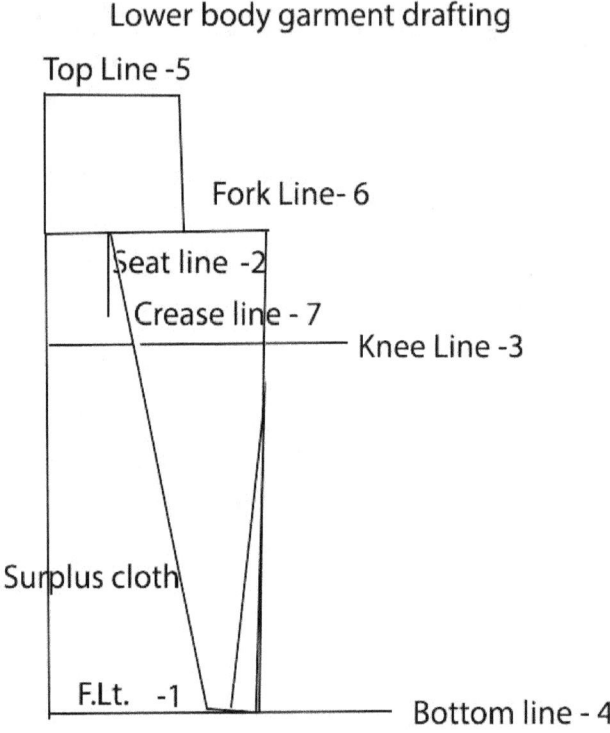

Lower body garment drafting

Now let us make one of these drafting blocks/patterns using some measurements. This is another method.

For this, we are taking the measurements of chest – **24 inches [60 cm],
height of waist – taken from the nape of the neck to the middle of the
waist – 11 inches and shoulders 13 cm – [5 inches].**

So let us start by making figure 1, which is going to start from **. 0**. Draw 0 –
1 – 2 with the help of the L-shaped ruler, and 0 – 5.

Here 1 – 0 is one fourth the measurement of the chest. 60 cm divided by 4 is
15 cm – 6 inches. 1 – 0 is going to be 6 inches. Mark that clearly.

2-0 is going to be the height of the waist from the nape of the neck to the
small of the waist/back somewhere around the middle of the spinal cord.

This is about 11 inches – 28 cm. Measure out 11 inches from 0 and mark it
.2 clearly.

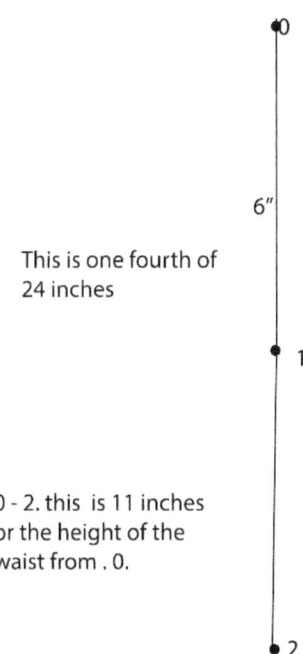

0 · 0

6"

This is one fourth of
24 inches

· 1

0 - 2. this is 11 inches
or the height of the
waist from . 0.

· 2

Now we are going to extend the lines widthwise.

You are going to say why I did not mark the points on the lines extended widthwise from 1 and 2 as 3 and 4. That is because 3 and 4 is reserved for the neck and the shoulder measurements.

So extend .8 and .9 from .1 and .2.

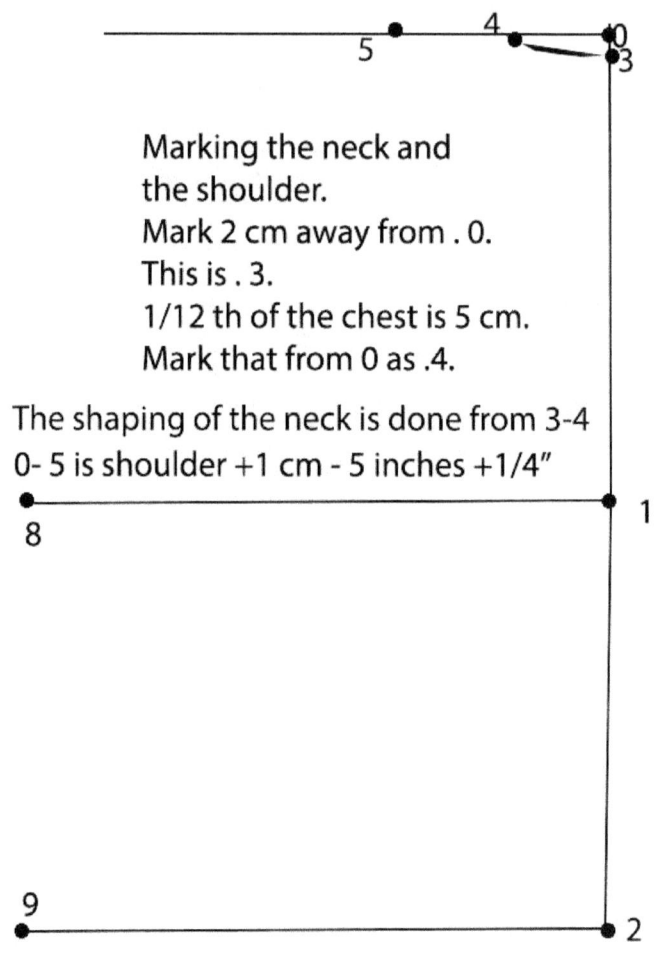

Marking the neck and
the shoulder.
Mark 2 cm away from . 0.
This is . 3.
1/12 th of the chest is 5 cm.
Mark that from 0 as .4.

The shaping of the neck is done from 3-4
0- 5 is shoulder +1 cm - 5 inches +1/4"

Now that we have shaped the neck, and measured the shoulder – 5 – it is time we drew lines from 5 to 6 to the line where we already have 1 and 8.

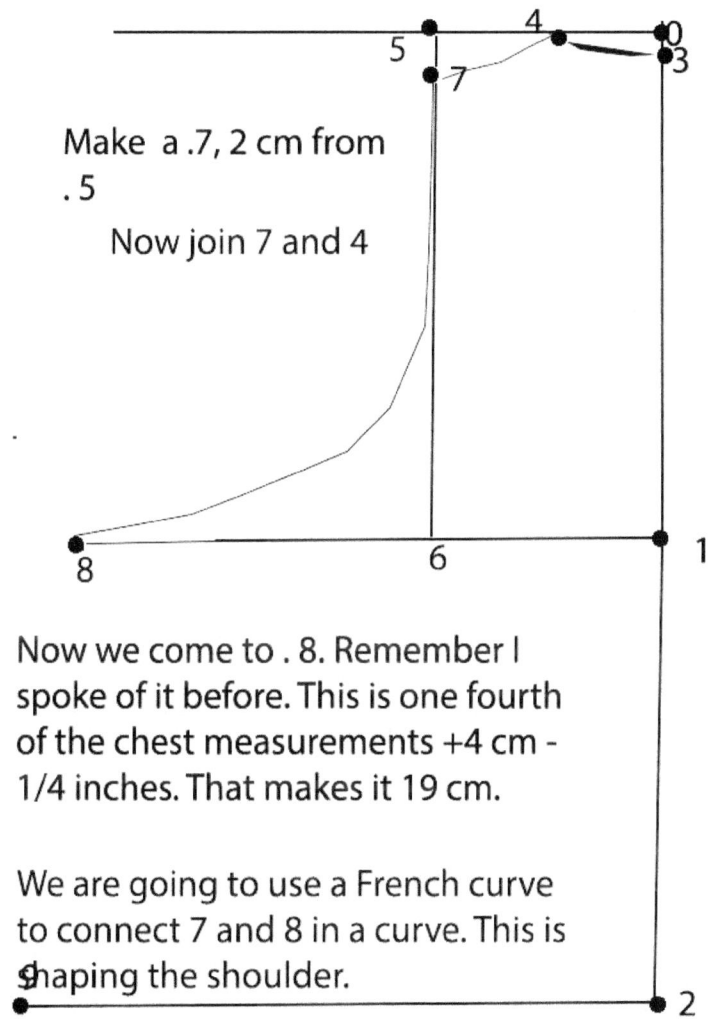

Make a .7, 2 cm from
.5

Now join 7 and 4

Now we come to . 8. Remember I spoke of it before. This is one fourth of the chest measurements +4 cm - 1/4 inches. That makes it 19 cm.

We are going to use a French curve to connect 7 and 8 in a curve. This is shaping the shoulder.

Remember to keep the curves properly rounded and smooth. They are not too smooth in the pictures given above, but as I am using designing software to make the sketches, on an Intuos tablet, I find designing curves a wobbly process! So bear with me. A proper draft designer, working on pen and paper is going to make a smooth curve with the French curves.

Now we are going to be shaping **the back of the bodice.**

Now we are going to make a line extending from 8 to 9. This is one fourth of the chest measurements +4 cm [1/2 inches.] Remember you measured, 8 from 1 with the same dimensions.

Measure the same from 2. When you draw a straight line from 8 to 9, both the points should meet.

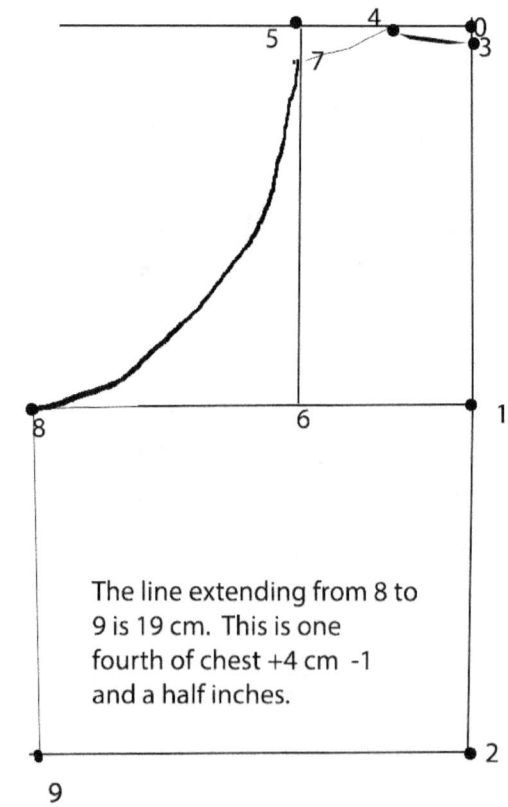

The line extending from 8 to 9 is 19 cm. This is one fourth of chest +4 cm -1 and a half inches.

Now we are going to make the darts. Those are easy. You are just going to measure 1 . 5 cm or half an inch from . 9 and market . 10. 9 and 10 is one half of the dart. This is how you have shaped the back of the bodice.

 Well Done! You have made your first draft by making a bodice pattern. Later on we are going to learn how to make patterns of other clothes, with common drafts.

You are going to ask why I have not used a tailor's dummy. How am I going to find a dummy which fits my exact measurements? Especially in the initial stages.

So we will forget about dummies at the moment, and the next volume is going to tell you how you can make more patterns, and alter existing patterns with more pattern practice.

So again, a recapitulation of all the measurements and how you are going to take them.

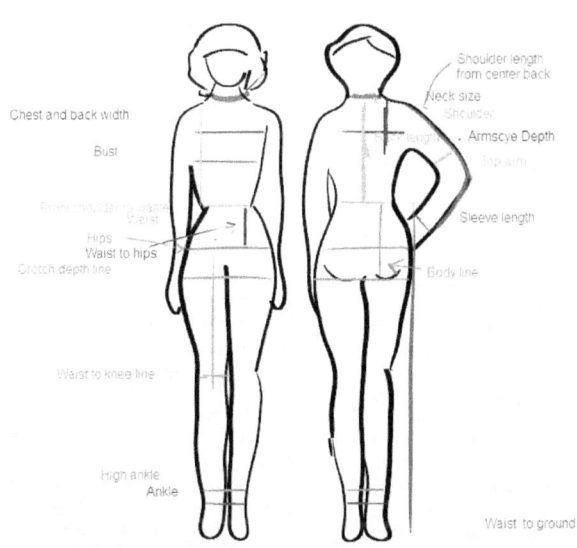

The leg measurements for around the thigh are taken around the fleshiest part of the thigh. The arm scye depth is from the middle of the neck to the chest, taken from the back. The back width and the chest width are taken together, front and back at the same time. This is a circular measurement like the bust measurement.

So there are usually 12 circular measurements – neck, chest [back width], bust, around the fullest part of the bust and the tape taken behind. The top arm measurement is taken in the fleshiest part of the arm, – biceps – with your arm bent – and the wrist is going to be around your wrist.

Waist, hips, crotch depth line and body line is taken from the hip –to the place where you sit and stand, measuring the fork. The body line is from the waist to that same place where your seat meets the surface on which you are sitting – taken from the back.

The thigh circumference, the knee line, the ankle line, the high ankle line, the mid-calf line, the small of leg line are all going to depend on the fitting of the garment, as is the sleeve length and the wrist measurements.

These are the normal measurements which cover all aspects of basic measuring. **The sleeve length is taken from the shoulder bone over the elbow to the wrist bone with your arm bent.**

The bust is the figure at the fullest point of the bust. The chest is normally 7 cm down from the neck point at the center front – armhole to armhole.

The shoulder is going to be from the neck to your shoulder bone.

Hips are measured in the widest part of the hips, approximately 21 cm from the waistline.

So the horizontal measurements are going to be the bust, the waist, the hips, the back width – 15 cm down from the neck bone/nape at the center back armhole to armhole, chest – when you are measuring the front 7 cm down from the neck point at the center front from armhole to armhole –, shoulder, neck size – from the base of the neck, touching the front collarbone both front and behind. – Top arm and wrist.

The vertical measurements are going to be from the waist. Just tie a string around the waist so that you know exactly where your waist falls naturally. If you have a stout figure, just stand straight and allow your elbows to tuck themselves in the natural point in the torso, on your body. The place where your elbow meets the waist is the point which you are going to measure. Tie a string around it.

The back neck to the waist is going to be from your neck bone/nape – this is the first bone of your spinal cord and is quite prominent and can be felt sharply protruding from underneath the skin – at the center back to the string tied around your waist.

Armhole depth is normally a standard measurement, which I showed you how you are going to calculate in previous volumes. There are different small armhole depth standard sizes in Germany, France, UK and US, so the calculation of the armhole depth from the neck to the beginning of the armpit will give you the armhole depth.

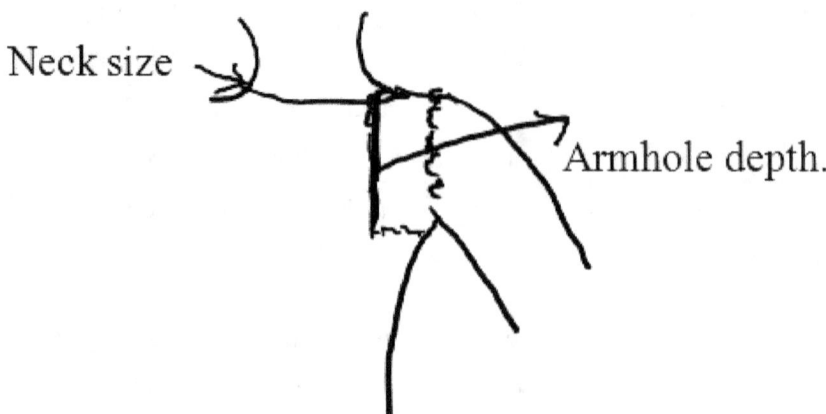

Neck size

Armhole depth.

We are going to make an ordinary short top blouse with these measurements –Length 40 ½ centimeters – 16 inches.

Chest – 81 cm [32 inches]
Waist – 71 cm [28 inches]
Neck – 38 cm [15 inches]
Shoulder – 33 cm [13 inches]
Sleeve – 20 ½ cm [8 inches]
Round of the sleeve – 23 cm [9 inches]

Drafting of the front portion of the blouse/bodice.
0 – 1 is the length – 40 ½ cms – 16 inches.
0 – 2 is 1/6 of the chest, +2 ½ centimeters [1 inch]= 16 ¼ centimeters approximately. [Approximately 6 ¼ inches.]
2 – 3= ¼ of chest +1 1/4 centimeters [half inch] equals to approximately 24 cm or 9 ½ inches.
0 – 4= half of the shoulder length [shoulder length/2]= 16 ½ centimeters [6 and a half inches.]
4 – 5 – straight line for joining

4 – 6 – 2 and a half centimeters.

6 – 3 – shaping of the front side of the armhole

0 – 7 – neck measurements/5 =7 ½ centimeters or 3 inches.

7 – 6 – straight line

0 – 8 – 12 ½ centimeters [5 inches] or according to your own choice. This is how you like your neck. Square, deep, round, or whichever design you prefer.

7 – 8 rounded/squared is going to be the shape of the neck from the front. I am going to Square it.

3 – 9 and 1 – 9= straight lines.

9 – 10 – 2 ½ centimeters – 1 inch.

3 – 10 – straight line

3 – 11= 12 ½ cm or 5 inches

From 11, you are going to put a slanting dart of 2 1/2 centimeters – 1 inch width and 12 and a half centimeters [5 inches] length.

12 is the center between 8 and 1. 8 to 12 and 12 to 1 are equidistant.

From 12, put a dart of 7 ½ centimeters – 3 inches length – and 1 ¼ centimeters ½ inches width.

These darts are going to be both on the right and left sides.

The distance between 1 to 13 and 13 – 10 is equal distance.

Make a dart here on 12 ½ centimeters – 5 inches length and 2 ½ cm – 1 inches width.

So we have drafted the first part – the front part of our bodice.

This is how it looks.

Front Part of the Bodice

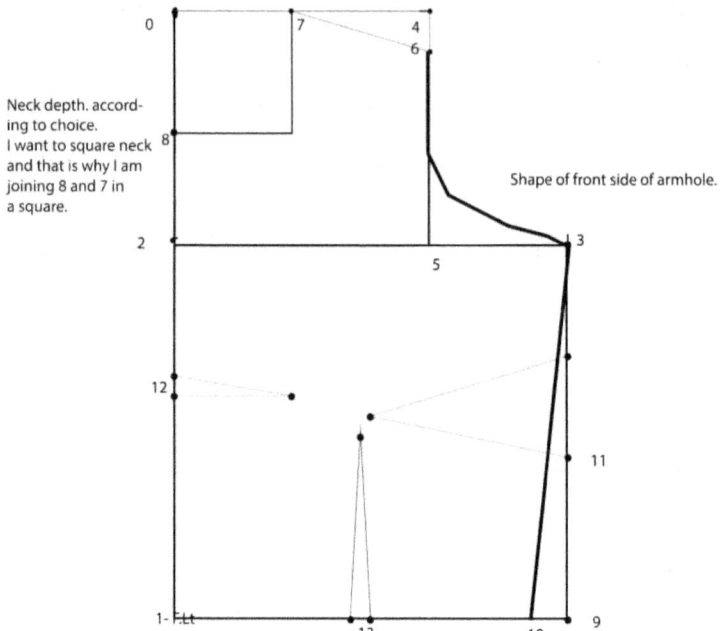

Neck depth. according to choice. I want to square neck and that is why I am joining 8 and 7 in a square.

Shape of front side of armhole.

Drafting the back portion is easier.

Back Part of the Bodice

0 – 1 is going to be different from the front. 16 inches minus 1 inch – makes it 38 cm or 15 inches.

0 – 2 is 1/6 of chest +2 ½ centimeters= 13 . 5 + 2 . 5 = 16 cm.

2 – 3= 81/4= 20 . 25 - 2 ½ centimeters= 17 . 7 5, but we are taking 18 cm or 7 inches which is a round figure.

0 – 4= shoulder length= 16 ½ centimeters [6 ½ inches]

4 – 5= straight line

4 – 6= 2 ½ cm [1 inch]

6 – 3= rounded shaping of the back portion armholes.

0 – 7= 1/5 of neck= 38= 7 . 6. CM, but I am taking 7 . 5 which is 3 inches.

7 – 6= straight line

0 – 8= 7 ½ centimeters [3 inches or according to choice]

7 – 8= shipping of the back portion of the neck

3 – 9, 1 – 9, 3 – 10= straight lines

1 – 11 is going to be the center of 1 to 10. That means one to 11 =11 to 10.

From 11-12, make a dart of 5 inches [12 ½ cm] length and 1 inch – 2 ½ centimeters – width.

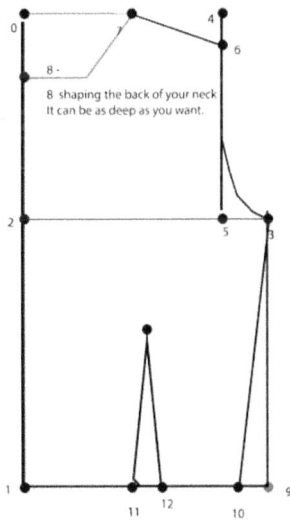

Sleeves

0 – 1= 16 cm [6 inches]

0 – 2= 20 1/2 cm [8 inches]

1 – 3 = 0 – 2

1 – 4= 7 ½ centimeters [3 inches]

2 – 5= ½ of sleeve round= 4 . 5 inches [11 ¼ cm]

4 – 5= straight line

0 – 4= shape of back and front side shoulder.

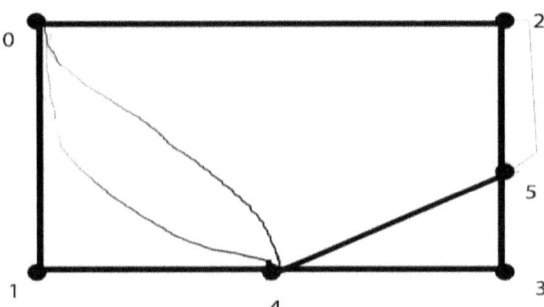

This is what a sleeve draft design is going to look like.

So now that we know more about the basics of pattern designing, the next volumes are going to talk about alteration of patterns, stitching, laying out the patterns, and other important tips about the basics of stitch craft and dress designing.

You may want to practice these designs and the designs to come, and one fine day we are going to stitch them, assemble them, and wear them with pride! As Time Goes by!

Author Bio

Dueep Jyot Singh is a Management and IT Professional who managed to gather Postgraduate qualifications in Management and English and Degrees in Science, French and Education while pursuing different enjoyable career options like being an hospital administrator, IT,SEO and HRD Database Manager/ trainer, movie , radio and TV scriptwriter, theatre artiste and public speaker, lecturer in French, Marketing and Advertising, ex-Editor of Hearts On Fire (now known as Solstice) Books Missouri USA, advice columnist and cartoonist, publisher and Aviation School trainer, ex-moderator on Medico.in, banker, student councilor ,travelogue writer … among other things!

One fine morning, she decided that she had enough of killing herself by Degrees and went back to her first love -- writing. It's more enjoyable! She already has 48 published academic and 14 fiction- in- different- genre books under her belt.

When she is not designing websites or making Graphic design illustrations for clients , she is browsing through old bookshops hunting for treasures, of which she has an enviable collection – including R.L. Stevenson, O.Henry, Dornford Yates, Maurice Walsh, De Maupassant, Victor Hugo, Sapper, C.N. Williamson, "Bartimeus" and the crown of her collection- Dickens "The Old Curiosity Shop," and "Martin Chuzzlewit" and so on… Just call her "Renaissance Woman" - collecting herbal remedies, acting like Universal Helping Hand/Agony Aunt, or escaping to her dear mountains for a bit of exploring, collecting herbs and plants, and trekking.

Check out some of the other JD-Biz Publishing books

Health Learning Series

THE MAGIC OF **GOOSEBERRIES** FOR HEALTH AND BEAUTY	THE MAGIC OF **YOGURT** FOR COOKING AND BEAUTY	THE MAGIC OF **LEMONS** USING LEMONS FOR HEALTH AND BEAUTY	THE MAGIC OF **CHILLIES** FOR COOKING AND HEALING	THE MAGIC OF **ONIONS** ONIONS IN CUISINE TO CURE AND TO HEAL	THE MAGIC OF **RADISHES** TO CURE AND TO HEAL
THE MAGIC OF **CARROTS** TO CURE AND TO HEAL	THE HEALTH BENEFITS OF **OREGANO** FOR COOKING AND HEALTH	The Magic Of **MARIGOLDS** Marigolds for Health And Beauty	THE HEALTH BENEFITS OF **CINNAMON**	THE MAGIC OF **COCONUTS** FOR COOKING & HEALTH	THE MAGIC OF **CLOVES** FOR HEALING AND COOKING
THE MAGIC OF **ASAFETIDA** FOR COOKING AND HEALING	THE MAGIC OF **NEEM** MARGOSA TO HEAL	THE MAGIC OF **SALT** TO HEAL AND FOR BEAUTY	THE MAGIC OF **POMEGRANATES** FOR HEALTH AND BEAUTY	THE MAGIC OF **DRY FRUIT AND SPICES** REMEDIES AND RECIPES	THE HEALTH BENEFITS OF **TURMERIC CURCUMIN** FOR COOKING AND HEALTH
THE MAGIC OF **ALOE VERA**	THE MAGIC OF **VEGETABLES** ANCIENT HEALING REMEDIES AND TIPS	THE HEALTH BENEFITS OF **ROSEMARY** FOR COOKING AND HEALTH	THE MAGIC OF **PEPPER & PEPPERCORNS** FOR COOKING & HEALING	THE MAGIC OF **MILK, BUTTER AND CHEESE** FOR COOKING & HEALING	THE MAGIC OF **CARDAMOMS** FOR COOKING AND HEALTH
THE HEALTH BENEFITS OF **BLACK CUMIN** FOR COOKING AND HEALTH	THE MAGIC OF **BASIL-TULSI** TO HEAL NATURALLY	THE MAGIC OF **SPICES** FOR HEALTH AND CUISINE	THE MAGIC OF **ROSES** FOR COOKING AND BEAUTY	The Miraculous Healing Powers of **GINGER**	The Miracle of **HONEY**

Country Life Books

Amazing Animal Book Series

Learn To Draw Series

How to Build and Plan Books

Entrepreneur Book Series

Our books are available at

1. Amazon.com

2. Barnes and Noble

3. Itunes

4. Kobo

5. Smashwords

6. Google Play Books

Download Free Books!

http://MendonCottageBooks.com

Publisher

JD-Biz Corp

P O Box 374

Mendon, Utah 84325

http://www.jd-biz.com/

Mendon Cottage Books

P O Box 374, Mendon Utah 84325

Mendon Cottage Books